Reaching New Levels of Faith

by
Curtis Hartshorn

WALKING IN HIS FOOTSTEPS PUBLICATIONS

214 S. Court
FARMINGTON, NEW MEXICO 87401

**Printed by
Walking In His Footsteps Publications**

REACHING NEW LEVELS OF FAITH

Table of Contents

Dedication

I am looking at my name on the front cover of this book and thinking of all the other names that should be there beside mine. Denny Petrillo and Jerry Palmer, who helped me with editing. My publisher, Fred Willmon, who also helped edit and did far more than merely print this book. There is Bill Stewart, one of my instructors from Bear Valley Bible Institute of Denver, who first encouraged me to put this material in book form. There is my lovely wife, Kathy. Next summer we will be celebrating our 20th anniversary. The ministry is not an easy life and she has stayed by my side, believing and encouraging me all the way. These names should be on the front cover along with others, but there is another individual I wish to dedicate this book to and that is my Dad. My Dad, Lloyd Curtis Hartshorn, passed away May 27, 2003. He did not get to see my book published. I wanted so much for him to hold this book in his big hands and relish each page and then tell me how proud he was of my work, which he did with every other accomplishment of my life. I write this with tears in my eyes, because Dad is gone, but he will live on inside of me. I will always be grateful for the values he instilled in me, and I dedicate this book to my father, Bud Hartshorn.

Reaching New Levels of Faith

"He who doubts is like a wave of the sea, blown and tossed by the wind" (James 1:6). Do you ever grow tired of doubting? There are times when I feel like a tiny boat whimsically tied to the shore of Christ. Waves of doubt are perpetually knocking against my hull and tugging at my feeble moorings. Have you ever felt that way? We flounder along through this journey we call Christianity, tossed back and forth because our faith is not solid. When we doubt God we start to rely on our own wisdom. That's when the big waves blind-side us. Life knocks us around. Satan gets us off course.

Parallel this verse with the one in Ephesians 4:14: "Then we will no longer be infants, tossed back and forth by the waves, and blown here and there by every wind of teaching and by the cunning and craftiness of men in their deceitful scheming." You've seen this happen, haven't you? A different wind of doctrine blows along and some of our number start chasing after it. To them it sounds fine, so they believe it until the next teaching comes along and then they chase that one. Back and forth they go, never growing up in their faith, no stability in their walk with God. This verse assures us there is a way to reach a point where this doctrinal battering no longer has an effect on us.

Shortly after my own conversion to Christ I began to wonder about why some Christians grow in their faith and some do not. My curiosity evolved into a near-obsession as I began researching and scouring the countryside probing the minds of those who were well known in their churches and communities for having strong faith. In 1988 I began teaching classes on this fascinating subject. I have taught seminars and classes on faith development in a number of churches while continuing my research at every opportunity. There is no question in my mind that this is a direly needed emphasis in our brotherhood.

Strong faith should be the aspiration of every Christian. Think of how much good could be accomplished with rock solid faith. Wouldn't it be great to have a faith like David or Moses or Joseph? Imagine a life of unwavering, unquestioning trust in the Almighty Creator of this universe. It tantalizes the spiritual taste buds. God the Father is searching the world over for souls who will trust Him. Hopefully this study will give you a vision for your own unlimited spiritual potential.

One reason we do not grow in our faith is because we do not understand the process of faith development. In order to blossom you must first be well rooted spiritually. As we begin to explore the various stages of faith development you will be able to determine exactly where you are in your walk with God. Once you discover that, you can know what steps to take next toward improving your confidence in God and His Word. Know this from the beginning: God never intended for His disciples to remain in a stagnant quagmire of mediocrity. God wants His children to grow and blossom spiritually. God truly wants you to reach new levels of faith.

Chapter One
Why Should I Develop My Faith?

In my limited travels I have encountered believers who consider it a waste of time to study or work on faith development. As far as they are concerned, they are saved and going to heaven and that is all that matters. On the other hand, there are many who long for a deeper relationship with the Father and are serious about doing everything they can to strengthen their faith. The fact that you are reading this book tells me you are most likely in the latter category. (Either that, or you are a friend or family member of mine just being supportive, in which case thank you for reading my book.) Whatever your reason is, I want to either give you a fresh motivation for growing in your trust in God or nurture the reason you already have. There are many *reasons* for working on our faith. Here are eight good ones.

First, I should want to grow in my faith because *God wants me to grow*. We know God wants us to grow because of the events recorded in Matthew 17. Jesus was up on the Mount of Transfiguration talking things over with Moses and Elijah. Although their conversation was a private one, I would love to have been invited. Two things are fascinating about this discussion. One is that these are three spiritual giants, the most faith-filled men the world has ever known. Just to be in their presence would have been awe-inspiring. The second thing that is fascinating about this scene is that during the time it takes place two of these three men have long been dead. Only three of the apostles were invited to witness this meeting. Where were the other nine? They were back in the city having an adventure of their own. Someone had brought them a boy who was demon possessed and having seizures. In Jesus' absence the apostles decided to step in and heal the boy themselves. It was a disaster. Their attempts to heal him failed which upset the boy's father, not to mention frustrating the daylights out of the apostles. It was about that time that Jesus returned from His journey.

"O unbelieving and perverse generation," Jesus replied, "how long shall I stay with you? How long shall I put up with you?" (17:17). Whether these words were directed toward his apostles, toward the assembly or toward that entire "generation" makes little difference. The point is He was obviously displeased with their lack of faith. We know this because after He rectified the situation and the crowds dispersed, the disciples approached Jesus hat-in-hand seeking understanding as to what went wrong. "Why couldn't we drive it out?" (17:19).

He replied, "Because you have so little faith," (17:20). The Greek word for "little faith" means tiny or puny faith, faith that is incredulous, a clear lack of confidence in God. The apostles are seeking an explanation and Jesus tells them exactly what the problem is, small faith. If your faith is miniscule there is very little you can do in the Christian realm because faith is the basis for it all. Jesus goes on to say, "I tell you the truth, if you have faith [ ] as a mustard seed, you can say to this mountain, 'move from here to there' and it will move" (17:20). In quoting this passage from the New International Version, you may notice I left out the words "as small". The reason is because the word "small" is not in the original Greek text. Only the Greek word which means "as, like or in comparison to" is used by the Holy Spirit. Jesus is drawing a comparison between faith and a mustard seed. The translators have emphasized the characteristic of smallness, which is understandable, but doing so disrupts the course of Jesus' point. He just rebuked them for having small faith. To turn around and tell them that with small faith they could move mountains alters His flow of instruction. No, the mustard seed comparison Jesus is making is not one of smallness but rather of growth.

We learn from Matthew 13:31-32 that although mustard seeds start off small they grow large enough to be considered as trees. The emphasis Jesus is making with His mustard seed illustration in Matthew 17 is not on being small in faith but that small faith should be growing. It does not matter how small our faith is when it starts out, but it does matter whether our faith is growing or not. Growing faith is what moves mountains. Growing faith is what God desires for His children. So, if I love God and God wants me to grow, I should want me to grow also. That alone is reason enough to work on our faith. We could stop here knowing we have reason enough to grow in our faith. But let's look at the other seven anyway.

A second good reason for working on our faith is when it comes to faith there are only two choices. *We are either moving forward or we are moving backward.* If I am not moving forward in my faith development I am moving backward - whether I realize it or not. We would like to think we are just "holding steady", but in principle this is impossible. If one is holding a steady level of faith, this is actually negative progress. The reason being, from the day we are baptized we should be growing up in the Lord. The Hebrew letter teaches us this.

> "We have much to say about this, but it is hard to explain because you are slow to learn. In fact, though by this time you ought to be teachers, you need someone to teach you the elementary truths of God's word all over again. You need milk, not solid food! Anyone who lives on milk, being still an infant, is not acquainted with the teaching about righteousness. But solid food is for the mature, who by constant use have trained themselves to distinguish good from evil." (Hebrews 5:11-14)

The statement "though by now you ought to be teachers" infers that there should be a steady progress of spiritual maturity among God's children. If that progress is not taking place in our lives, then we are in fact digressing. Christians should be continually training themselves to get off the milk and on to solid food. If a child stopped growing physically, you would not think, "Well, at least he is not shrinking!" would you? No, that's crazy. You would be alarmed that the natural process of growth had been disrupted, especially if it was your own child. That is how God feels when He sees a child of His that has stopped growing spiritually.

The third reason for working on our faith is that *life is boring without growth*. I have met some Christians who thought that Christianity was boring. You may have as well, but have you ever met a growing Christian who thought that Christianity was boring? I'll bet not. I certainly have not. Challenging, maybe. Difficult, possibly. But never boring. "For the word of God is living and active" (Hebrews 4:12). Anyone who is growing in the Word is active and drinking deeply of life. Growth is what makes life lively. The very process of overcoming obstacles as we move toward a closer walk with God is what gives life that pizzazz. Growth is exciting. It is fun. It can even be scary at times, but never boring.

A fourth reason for working on our faith is that it is essential for a growing church. *Without spiritual growth we cannot have numerical growth in our congregations*, at least not a sustained numerical growth. It is possible to grow in numbers for a while without growing spiritually, but if you do not have spiritual maturity taking place in your congregation there will not be a strong enough base to sustain all the new Christians. "From him the whole body, joined and held together by every supporting ligament, grows and builds itself up in love, as each part does its work" (Ephesians 4:16). Eventually the numbers drop back to where they were, if the body has not developed the necessary supporting ligaments. Churches that emphasize spiritual growth along with numerical growth have a lasting impact on their community because they are staying attached to the vine (John 15:1-17). If adding souls to the kingdom of God means anything to you then spiritual growth has to be part of the game plan.

This fifth reason for working on our faith has to do with the realization that we are involved in a spiritual battle. Like it or not, there is a spiritual war competing for our eternal destinies. And in this war we are in one army or we are in the other. This is hard for us to accept. Many of us have had tolerance and neutrality preached to us from birth. We resist taking sides under any circumstances, but in this instance we have no choice. The cold hard fact is that *if God does not get you, Satan will.* Peter once gave this exhortation: "Humble yourselves, therefore, under God's mighty hand, that he may lift you up in due time. Cast all your anxiety on him because he cares for you," (1 Peter 5:6-7). In simple terms Peter is urging us to enlist in God's army. Why? Because . . . "Your enemy the devil prowls around like a roaring lion looking for someone to devour" (5:8). We are either on God's team or the devil's team. Jesus challenged His disciples, "He who is not with me is against me, and he who does not gather with me scatters," (Matthew 12:30). John explained in 1 John 3:7-10 that we can either be children of God or we can be children of the devil. There is no neutrality in this battle. One reason for growing in our faith is so that we can stay out of Satan's camp.

Reason number six: *without faith we can't even please God* (Hebrews 11:6). Do you want to please God? I know you do. This is what we as Christians live for. We long to know that our heavenly Father is proud of the lives we are living, but we can not please God without faith. The Bible says it is impossible. God loves to see faithfulness. It pleases Him to see men and women aspiring to have a deeper trust in Him.

The seventh reason for faith development is so that our churches will grow. *If I want a healthy, vibrant church I have to start with me.* This is what is wrong with so many churches today. Everyone wants to be part of a strong congregation, but we think the way to attain that is for everyone else to get their lives straightened out. It is always somebody else's fault. The best thing you can do for your congregation is work on you. Do you want your church to be strong? Start with strengthening your own faith. *"From him the whole body, joined and held together by every supporting ligament, grows and builds itself up in love, as EACH PART DOES ITS WORK"* (Ephesians 4:16) [Emphasis mine].

The last of the eight reasons for spiritual maturity is that *it makes one more useful to the Lord in dealing with the brethren.* This discovery was the serendipitous result of the first few seminars I did. After following up with some of the congregations where we had implemented this program, several church leaders told me that they had realized an increase in patience among the members with one another, which they attributed to our study together. It wasn't hard to figure out why. The patience came from finally understanding the struggles that other members were going through. Members started to realize how hard it was for others to grow from one level of faith to another, or what it was like to go through some of the struggles they had learned about. By focusing their attention on the progress of spiritual maturity, these brethren learned to feel for one another. This alone can be a motivation for trying to grow in our faith. By working together on our spiritual growth we will foster harmony in our brotherhood.

Take a moment to look back over these eight reasons for growing in God. Somehow you need to find a motivation for wanting to grow closer to God. It may be through one or more of these reasons or by coming up with your own, but somehow you need to find a godly reason for wanting spiritual maturity in your life. So many Christians never progress spiritually because of a lack of righteous motivation. Any relationship takes time, effort and determination. There are plenty of reasons for you to work on strengthening your walk with God. Choose one and get motivated!

Discussion Questions

1. Can you list the 8 reasons given in this chapter for working on our faith?

2. Why do you think some Christians are not motivated to want to develop more faith?

3. Can you see how it is God's desire for you to be growing in your faith?

4. How does growth take the boredom out of life?

5. What is going to be your personal motivation for wanting to grow in your faith?

Chapter Two

What Is Faith?

Since we are going to be talking a great deal about faith in this book, it makes sense that we should get a firm grasp on just what faith is. But before looking at some definitions, think about how you would define it. What is your concept of faith? How would you explain it to a friend? Does faith mean to accept an idea without question? Is faith just about going to church, reading your Bible and praying? Contrary to popular opinion, faith is not the blind acceptance of unfounded fables. *Faith is trust based on previous evidence.* True faith is something that is tried and tested. It is based on reasonable evidence which supports the conclusion. I have faith that if I put my hand on the stove it will burn my hand. This faith is based on the evidence of past experiences which have led me to this conclusion. Out of personal embarrassment I would rather not go into the details of how I know a stove will burn my hand. Let us suffice it to say, my faith is based on the evidence. I have seen (and felt) what a stove is capable of doing! Likewise, I have faith in God based on what I have seen Him do in my life and in the lives of those around me. Where other methods have failed, God's way of doing things has worked. Witnessing this strengthens my faith in God.

Faith is the absence of doubt. You can't make yourself believe something without addressing the issues you have doubts about. A friend once told me, "A man persuaded against his will is of the same persuasion still." You can make yourself do some things you ought to do but if you keep thinking in the back of your mind that it is all a waste of time, you will find it hard to stay on the right path. Doubts start coming into your mind and you begin to believe those doubts. When you believe your doubts, then you start doubting your beliefs. You need to doubt your doubts and then, after conquering those doubts, you will be free to believe your beliefs. (Please don't ask me to say that again.)

Faith is putting your full weight down upon something. The story is told of a missionary working with a secluded tribe of natives. They had no translation of the Bible in their language so the missionary set out to provide them with one. As he began putting the Bible into their words, he discovered that they did not have an equivalent for the word "faith" in their native tongue. One day while traveling through the forest they came to a bridge made of twisted grass ropes. They had to make sure it was safe to cross so one person carefully tested it by gradually putting more and more weight on it. When he put his full weight on the bridge they had a word for that and the missionary thought, "Aha, that's the word I've been looking for." Their translation of the Bible reads something like this in John 2:11: "This, the first of his miraculous signs, Jesus performed in Cana of Galilee. He thus revealed his glory and his disciples put their [full weight down upon] him." What an insightful way to think about the concept of faith.

Faith is the conviction of a religious truth. If there is anything lacking in the Lord's church today it is people of conviction. God needs men and women with a passion for the cause of Christ. He has enough pew warmers already. In the church we have lots of beliefs, but not enough belief. God needs men and women who are not afraid to roll up their sleeves and step up to the challenge of defending the truth.

Faith is reliance upon Christ. Whenever we worry about our problems, or we struggle along trying to handle life in our own way, we lack faith. It takes true faith to accept Jesus' invitation to come to him when we are weak and burdened (Matthew 11:28). It is not easy to leave our worries at the foot of the cross and let the Lord guide us. Deep down we know that relying on Jesus, instead of our own wisdom, is the wisest way to handle our problems. But it is easier said than done, isn't it?

The Bible says in Hebrews 11:1, "Now faith is being sure of what we hope for and certain of what we do not see." Is faith a blind acceptance of things that deep down we do not honestly believe? No, it's being "SURE of what we hope for." What do we as Christians hope for? I have the hope that God can change my life. When I am unsure about whether God could ever change me, I am displaying a lack of faith. Paul once wrote to the church in Corinth, "Do you not know that the wicked will not inherit the kingdom of God?" (1 Corinthians 6:9). He went on to list sins like sexual immorality, male prostitution, homosexuality and drunkenness. Then he said, "And that is what some of you were" (6:11). Notice that he uses the past tense "were". That means they used to be involved in those sins but they were not anymore. If God can rescue all these Corinthians from such ungodly backgrounds, He can change me too. I can be sure of that.

I also need to be sure that God can change others. Do you know anyone so steeped in sin it is difficult to imagine them ever following God? If you said to yourself, "So-and-so could never change," that is a faithless statement. Our faith demands that we see people for what they can become and not merely for what they are. I was sitting in a court room a few months ago while a judge was reviewing the case on an inmate who was up for reconsideration. The judge told him, "I see that you have put in a request for rehabilition, but it is obvious from your record that you are unrehabilitatible." I wanted to scream when I heard that. No matter what someone has done, there is always hope because there is always God. Remember Paul when he prayed for the Philippians, "being confident of this, that he who began a good work in you will carry it on to completion until the day of Christ Jesus" (Philippians 1:6).

If we are to be sure of what we hope for, we need to be sure that life in Christ is the best life available to mankind. Returning to our chapter in Hebrews eleven we read in verse six: "And without faith it is impossible to please God, because anyone who comes to him must believe that he exists and that he rewards those who earnestly seek him." We generally have no problem believing that God exists, but do you believe that God rewards those who are seeking him? Faith involves understanding that there is a God who is greater than any of our problems. Even though we will have our share of rough times, God is steadily improving the lives of those who are steadily moving closer to Him. You can be sure of that too.

Faith is not just "being sure of what we hope for," but also being "certain of what we do not see." Having faith involves an acceptance of a realm that cannot be seen. Not only are we to acknowledge it, we are to be "certain" that it exists. There should be no doubt there is a God in heaven who cares about each of us personally. We also need to have confidence that He has an eternal dwelling prepared for us, just as He promised in His Word. We need to be certain we believe in Satan. If we do not believe in him we make a critical tactical error in our war against evil. Satan is very real and active in this world today. The evidence of that is abundant. Believe in the unseen.

Hopefully by now you have a good working knowledge of what faith is and what it is not. This will become vitally important as you begin to understand where you are right now in your walk with God and as you set goals to increase your faith. You now have a motivation for working on your faith and you have a basic understanding of what faith is. Now you are ready to study the progression of faith in the life of the Christian.

Discussion Questions

1. Do you feel like you had a good biblical concept of what faith truly is before you read this chapter?

2. If not, do you have any idea how your erroneous concept of faith got started and can you see any impact it has had on your walk with God?

3. Do you see the connection between faith and conviction?

4. Do you struggle with having faith in something you cannot see or touch?

5. In your own words, what is faith?

Chapter Three
What Are the Different Levels of Faith?

As Christians growing in our walk with the Lord, there are basically five levels of faith that we progress through. Think of them as stages of life. We start with infancy and move on to the toddler stage, then there is preadolescence, adolescence, etc. In the same way we pass through various stages of our faith. These five levels are Imitating Faith, Affiliating Faith, Searching Faith, Solidifying Faith and Mature Faith. To begin with, we want to learn the terminology of each level and show the scriptural basis for all five of them. Starting in the next chapter we can examine each one in greater detail.

The most basic level of faith is what is called ***Imitating Faith***. Those with Imitating Faith are learning by following the example of others. They really don't understand the whys and wherefores. They watch and imitate. This is the faith of a child wanting to take the Lord's Supper because he sees others doing it, wanting to put a dollar in the offering plate because others do. This is faith, but it is faith at its most unpretentious level.

Imitating Faith is the most difficult one to find in the Bible because it is essentially a child's faith. Rarely would an adult start at this level, but if anyone in the Bible exhibited these qualities it was Simon the Sorcerer. While in Samaria he had the opportunity to hear Philip preach and watch him perform miracles, real miracles. After watching Philip baptize several of the Samaritans into Christ the text says, "Simon himself believed and was baptized" (Acts 8:13). The main distinction between Imitating and Affiliating Faith is that with Imitating Faith there is little understanding of the purpose behind the actions. Simon appears not to have fully understood the driving motivation behind Christian behavior, because later in the text when Peter and John were imparting the miraculous manifestations of the Holy Spirit through the laying on of their hands, Simon offered to pay them for it. Clearly he did not understand what he was doing or he would not have made such an audacious request, one for which Peter rebuked him strongly (8:20-23). Simon had a very simple faith. It was still faith, but it was faith at its most rudimentary level.

The next step up is called *Affiliating Faith*. At this level there is a basic understanding of why things are done, but it is still a copy faith. It is faith based on who one affiliates with, rather than being based on one's own seeking process. The faith is not really owned. It is borrowed from others.

Affiliating Faith is easy enough to see in the first century Christians. One of the better examples lies in the Gospel of John. As a result of conversing with Christ about living water in chapter four, the Samaritan woman came to believe in Him and returned to her village to tell her family and friends about Jesus. They acquired enough faith through their affiliation with her that they were willing to investigate it for themselves. She led them to Christ through her affiliation with them, but once they met Christ personally the text says, "We no longer believe just because of what you said; now we have heard for ourselves, and we know that this man really is the Savior of the world" (4:42). Affiliating Faith is the best way to lead someone to Christ. You most likely came to Christ through your affiliation with a parent, friend, teacher or preacher. But it is important that we do not stay at this immature stage. These Samaritan towns-people went on to search out the basis for their faith.

Today many Christians are trapped in Affiliating Faith and it is impeding the growth of God's kingdom. Allow me to illustrate this condition for you. Imagine that you are an Affiliate Believer tied with an imaginary rope to another believer who is in turn tied to Christ. It is okay to become a Christian through an affiliation of some kind. Most of us do. But as long as you stay in this position, there is a buffer between you and Jesus keeping you from having a deep personal relationship with the Savior. The believer between you and Jesus cannot grow as well because they have to concentrate on the tie they have with you. This in-between disciple also cannot reach out to others as well for the same reason. You are also not likely to reach out to others either because you are not closely tied to Jesus. (Affiliating Believers are rarely evangelistic.) There is also a danger because if the in-between believer moves away, or worse yet, falls away, you are going to have a struggle not to fall away yourself. Have you ever watched as a preacher leaves a congregation and several members stop attending? Most likely their relationship with God was dependent on their affiliation with the preacher. Christians should not have their relationships with Christ dependent on the spiritual well being of others. Each one should search out his or her own faith.

The third level of faith is *Searching Faith*. This is when we reach the point where we start investigating and seeking out what we believe for ourselves. Searching Faith breaks us out of the comfort zone because we are struggling to find out why we believe what we believe.

Many biblical characters exemplify Searching Faith. The Bereans in Acts 17 were commended because they "examined the Scriptures every day to see if what Paul said was true" (17:11). This is the very definition of Searching Faith. Their level of maturity was such that they did not base their faith merely on the affiliation they had with Paul and Silas. They pursued the truth to the point it became their very own. Young Christians will do this naturally if we allow them to. The problem is Searching Faith is often squelched by well-intentioned church peers and parents. Searching Faith looks like doubt because the young believer is questioning so many things. But if they are not allowed to search they may try to find another church where they can search out their faith. Some religious groups may allow them the flexibility to believe what they want to believe, but without the guidance to stay within the perimeters of God's Word. If not encouraged to search, some might give up and settle for Affiliating Faith. Or worse yet, they may abandon their faith altogether. None of these choices are good ones. That is why it is essential that we learn how to distinguish Searching Faith from spiritual digression and provide each Christian in our congregation with the environment to *"work out[their] salvation with fear and trembling"* (Php. 2:12).

The fourth level is ***Solidifying Faith***. There comes a point where the believer has searched through all the evidence and needs to start piecing it together. We start arriving at some conclusions about what we believe and our faith begins to solidify. As we study more you will begin to see how vitally important this step is.

Timothy is a worthy example of Solidifying Faith. His Searching led him to where he needed to solidify his understanding of who God is and what he wants from him. Even though we never stop searching out the truths of God's Word, it is essential that we eventually piece together (make solid) the evidences before us. Timothy's faith was not quite mature but he had many godly attributes. His faith was sincere. Paul commends him for it in 2 Timothy 1:5. Just as Paul exhorts him to "fan into flame" his spiritual gift (1:6), we must also fan our faith into flame. Anyone who has tried to ignite a piece of paper with a dashboard cigarette lighter can relate to Paul's illustration. The paper just smokes and smolders until you fan it or blow on it. Timothy had been searching out his faith under the careful tutelage of Paul, but now it was time to focus his search and piece together evidences he had uncovered. It was time to solidify his faith. There are other biblical examples we will look at later on.

The final level of faith is ***Mature Faith***. This should be the goal of every Christian. As we will see in our biblical examples, Mature Faith does not mean that one is "sinlessly" perfect. It is simply reaching that level of trust where nothing or no one can dissuade you from doing the will of the Lord.

For an example of Mature Faith, there are also a number of biblical characters we could consider. Paul is one of the easiest to identify because we can see how his faith grew from the day of his conversion. His faith grew like a mustard seed to the point he was fully mature. Toward the end of Paul's life when he was under arrest and being taken by ship to Rome to stand trial, the ship he was on was caught in a furious storm that lasted several days. Everyone on the ship lost hope of being saved, except for Paul. He reassured the others saying, "Last night an angel of the God whose I am and whom I serve stood beside me and said, 'Do not be afraid, Paul'" (Acts 27:23-24). The confidence with which Paul faced tribulation speaks volumes about the maturity level of his faith. So does his statement about "the God whose I am and whom I serve." Paul knew who he belonged to and who he was serving. This comes through having mature faith. Paul was not perfect, but nothing was going to dissuade him from obeying his Master.

These five levels of faith will be the backbone of our study. It would be helpful for you to take a few minutes to memorize them and learn the basic meaning of each one. If you look through the scriptures you will find many other examples. I would encourage you to do so. The more you work with this model the more comfortable it will become and the more you will be able to accomplish with it in helping yourself and helping others progress to a deeper faith. Continually refer back to your motivation for doing this study. How much you get out of this study is based on your own desire for a deeper relationship with your Lord and Savior.

Discussion Questions

1. Practice saying the five levels of faith until you can say them all without looking.

2. What level of faith do you believe you are at right now?

3. Have you ever been discouraged from Searching out your faith or have you ever discouraged someone else from Searching?

4. If you have children, how can you encourage them to Search out their own convictions without them drifting from the path of sound doctrine?

5. Is it possible to be at different levels of faith in different aspects of your Christianity at the same time?

Chapter Four

How Do I Graduate From Imitating Faith?

As we witnessed in the example of Simon the Sorcerer, it is possible for an adult to have Imitating Faith, but for the most part Imitating Faith belongs to the children. Most everyone reading this book will not be at the Imitating Faith level, but your children might be or other children that you are working with. So we should take a moment to look at how to assist a child during this stage of faith.

If your child is at the stage of Imitating Faith there are four ways you can help them develop their own faith. First, *watch for opportunities to teach them* why you believe what you believe and why you do the things you do. Children are naturally curious. When they want to know about the Lord's Supper tell them what it means and why we participate in this memorial. Look for opportunities to teach them about the fundamentals of the Christian faith.

Recently, while we were having breakfast, my 10 year old son was telling us the latest rumors about who liked who at school. He had been asked to pass notes back and forth for those too shy to talk face to face. We talked about some of the problems that arise from dating at too early an age. We talked about gossip and how listening was as wrong as repeating certain things we have heard about others. We also talked about the risk of being the middle person in any relationship and encouraged him to let people deliver their own messages when they had something to say. Over breakfast an opportunity arose to teach our son three valuable life skills. We shared with him what the Bible taught about these and other topics and tried to nurture his faith and encourage his questions.

Next, *focus on learning rather than teaching*. The education of your child does not depend as much on how well you are teaching them, but rather how well they are learning. Study your child's learning strengths and tailor your education methods to fit your child. Share your findings with your child's Bible class teachers and ask them if they would help your child to get more out of each lesson by implementing these techniques.

Thirdly, **nurture your child's natural hunger for learning God's Word**. Read the Bible together with your children. Watch movies based on the Bible and discuss them with each other. Find a good dramatized version of the Bible on cassettes or CDs and listen to them for family night once a week. The greatest gift you can give your child is a knowledge of God's Word. If they know the Word for themselves their faith can grow past the Imitating stage.

Finally, **make worship services as enjoyable as possible**. How many people do you know who don't want to go to church because when they were young their parents "made them go." What they are saying is that church was a drudgery. Church meant fussing around Sunday morning trying to get ready. It was a hassle getting there and they couldn't wait to leave when it was over. It was a place where they had to sit still on hard pews with their eyes facing forward all the time. If they turned around to look at something, they had their little heads turned back to the front. The whole service was something for their parents and not for them. Does church really have to be that way for children?

Matthew 22:2 says, "The kingdom of heaven is like a king who prepared a wedding banquet for his son." Jesus is describing the kingdom, which is made up of everyone who is subject to the king. That's us, Christians. And when Christians get together to worship the King it should be a joyful occasion like a great wedding feast. Christianity is something to be enjoyed, not endured. Is your child getting that message or are they getting another message entirely? Teach your children to participate in the singing and prayer. Doing so will lend meaning and purpose to what they are doing. Let them know that church is for them too. You do not want your child to be unruly and distracting to others, but allow them some leeway whenever possible to change positions and look around at what others are doing. Find ways to make the church service a positive experience for your child and nurture their desire to know God for themselves.

Teaching our children about God is one of the most important jobs we have in the Lord's church. These young souls are so precious. If we want them to carry on the Lord's work after we are gone we must show them that Christianity is a gift they can treasure for a lifetime.

Discussion Questions

1. What is the difference between Imitating and Affiliating Faith?

2. Have you recently had an opportunity to teach a child something about your faith? How did you handle it?

3. If you have children, would you say your child learns best by seeing, hearing or feeling? How can you use this knowledge to help them learn?

4. What can you do to help your child learn God's Word?

5. Do the children in your congregation enjoy going to church? What can you do to make it more enjoyable without being disruptive to other members?

Chapter Five

How to Recognize Affiliating Faith

Spotting Affiliating Faith within yourself should be easy enough to do. If you believe what you believe because others believe it, you have Affiliating Faith. All it takes is some honesty with yourself and you can tell whether you are an Affiliate believer or not. But seeing Affiliating Faith in other believers is more challenging because we have to rely on external signs. Jesus could see into people's hearts and know what was going on in their minds. We have to rely on the peripheral signs to determine where another disciple is in their walk with God. For that reason we are going to learn the external indicators of Affiliating Faith.

There are three basic external signs that help us to recognize Affiliating Faith in one of Jesus' followers. The first is **monotonous prayer**. Affiliate believers lack freshness and spontaneity in their conversation with the Creator. Their prayers are repetitious to the point you can usually guess what they are going to say next. You can tell by listening to them pray that their walk with God lacks intimacy. Jesus told us, "And when you pray, do not keep on babbling like the pagans, for they think they will be heard because of their many words," (Matthew 6:7).

The Greek word for "babbling" means to utter empty words, vain repetitions, to repeat the same thing over and over. Jesus warned us not to do this and yet some denominations today encourage repetitious prayer to the detriment of their members. They teach rote sayings to be mindlessly uttered during a worship service or in individual worship. Doing so inhibits the worshipper from having a more personal relationship with their Father.

In this same passage some have taken the example prayer that Jesus gave to us, known as the Lord's Prayer, and used it for what Jesus just warned us against. Jesus said in Matthew 6:9, "This, then, is HOW you should pray," [emphasis mine], not, "This, then, is WHAT you should pray." Memorizing Jesus' prayer is good but repeating it over and over to God does not make any sense. God doesn't need to hear it over and over. He wants to hear our personal, sincere thoughts. Prayer is just talking to God. Since Affiliative believers are not searching out a deeper relationship with the Father, they prefer memorized prayers. Affiliating believers are also not likely to pray about things that are beyond the realm of human possibility. Their faith is often too shallow to ask God to do something that is supernatural.

The second sign of Affiliating Faith is **resistance to change** of any kind. Mature Christians will resist changes that are unscriptural. But Christians whose faith is based on affiliation have their faith based on familiarity, thus even scriptural change appears to be a threat.

Jesus told the Pharisees that you cannot pour new wine into old wineskins (Mark 2:22). When Jesus started changing the way things were done in Israel, the Pharisees were the first to voice their objection. Guess what kind of faith the Pharisees had. The system by which the Pharisees received their training fits the description of what we are calling Affiliating Faith. Every Pharisee went through an exhaustive training period under a faculty of Jewish scholars known as the Tannaim. Rabbinical oral traditions had been passed down and finally recorded in scrolls known as the Mishnah. The Pharisees were taught from the Mishnah rather than directly from God's Word and they were discouraged from searching the scriptures for themselves. If they had searched the scriptures, they would have recognized Jesus as the coming Messiah and welcomed his changes. Instead, they saw Jesus' teaching as a contradiction to their comfortable traditions and opposed Him from day one.

In the same way, Affiliate believers in our day oppose change of any kind. Why? Because they have not studied through what they believe enough to be comfortable with any variance from the norm. If you want to find out who has Affiliating Faith in your congregation, just change the order of the worship service. Have four prayers instead of three. Have the Lord's Supper after the sermon instead of before. Announce that next Sunday the congregation is meeting at 3:00 in the afternoon instead of 11:00 in the morning. You will soon find out who knows why they believe the things they believe.

The third external indicator of Affiliating Faith is **canned comments**. Here are some examples of canned comments to common church questions. "What is a parable?" "An earthly story with a heavenly meaning." "What is faith?" "The evidence of things hoped for; the assurance of things not seen." "What is the gospel?" "The death, burial and resurrection." Affiliate believers rely on regurgitated answers to typical Bible questions because for them no searching is taking place outside of the church assemblies. That is where their affiliative foundation lies. These canned answers are correct for the most part, but the problem with them is that they can be mindlessly repeated without any real learning taking place. Those with more mature faith are able to come up with freshly insightful comments in the class setting. By listening to the comments that are made in Bible classes and group Bible studies you can tell who is spending time in God's Word strengthening their relationship with the Creator, and who is merely repeating what they have been told.

By using these three indicators you will be able to tell who has Affiliating Faith. This ability can be productive but it can also be detrimental if you use it the wrong way. Whatever you do, do not exploit this information by branding or pigeon-holing people. This knowledge is not so we can have labels to faction the church with. I am teaching you this terminology so that we can have a working knowledge of what we are trying to accomplish. Working in the field of spiritual maturity requires a constant evaluation of our own motives. Use this knowledge to do good and not harm.

Discussion Questions

1. How do you know if you have Affiliating Faith?

2. What are the three outward signs that someone you are working with has Affiliating Faith?

3. What kind of faith did the Pharisees have?

4. Why do Affiliating believers resist change?

5. Without looking, can you list the five different levels of faith?

Chapter Six

How Do I Acquire Searching Faith?

One of the most rewarding benefits of this study is the way it reinforces the basics of the Christian faith. As a Christian you have been urged to go to church, read your Bible, pray, and have fellowship with others in the church. Reaching New Levels of Faith provides you with a reason for doing all these things. Remember your motivation that we talked about in the first chapter. Know why you want to grow in your faith. It is not enough just to say you have faith. The Jews that Jesus spoke to in John 8:31 "believed Him." They had faith, but when He admonished them to search out the truth and know it, they rejected the deeper faith He was offering and wanted to kill him (v. 37). What happened to their faith? They didn't want to break out of their comfort zones and find out the truth about how shallow their relationship with God truly was. Consequently they never experienced the freedom that comes from knowing the truth (v. 32). It may be time for you to venture out on the limb a little and take a closer look at just how close you are with God.

Many of the participants at the workshops I have done find out that they have Affiliating Faith and they want to move on to a higher spiritual plain. If that is the position you find yourself in, here is what I recommend that you do. First ask yourself three questions.

1. Put foremost in your mind the person who has the greatest impact on you spiritually. It could be a church leader, a parent, a spouse, the person who led you to Christ . . . Now ask yourself, **"If this person stopped coming to church, would I keep going?"** Perhaps it is inconceivable to you that this person could walk away from the Lord, but that's not the point. If they did lose their conviction to follow God, could you go on without them? As harsh as this might

sound, you have to put yourself in a position so that your relationship with Jesus is not dependent on the spiritual well being of any other individual. That doesn't mean you don't need other Christians involved in your life. You do need others or God would not have designed the church. But if your walk with God depends on another soul's walk with God, you are easy pickings for Satan. Prepare yourself to press forward no matter what others may do.

2. Ask yourself this question: **"I know what I believe, but do I know why I believe it?"** Have you honestly thought through what your beliefs are based on? Until you are willing to examine the doctrines you hold to and own them for yourself, you will continue to have Affiliating Faith.

3. Ask yourself, **"Am I willing to change what I believe if the Bible says differently?"** Our own stubborn pride is what prevents us from growing up spiritually as we should. We hate to admit when we are wrong. If you are confident that God's Word is right and it contradicts what you believe, then guess what? You need a faith lift.

After you have dealt with these three questions, you are ready to start moving forward in your Searching Faith. The greatest single thing you could do to strengthen your faith is to learn to share it with others. In all my years as a Christian I have not found a better way to get young Christians to grow than by encouraging them to talk to others about Christ. When Paul was spiritually nurturing his comrade Philemon he told him, "I pray that you may be active in sharing your faith, so that you will have a full understanding of every good thing we have in Christ" (Philemon 1:6). When we begin sharing what we believe with others, we often find ourselves having to confirm our beliefs to them. This causes us to search.

When I was a young Christian in college I was trying to reach out to a classmate and encourage him to come to church with me. He told me that he believed God was in his heart, and that he didn't need to go to church to worship God. Well, I really didn't have a good answer for that at the time. I had to go back to God's Word and search out the purpose of attending church services. Sharing your faith makes you search, which causes you to grow. Whether we are talking spiritually or physically, feeding others is a sign of true maturity. When you have participated in leading a lost soul to Jesus, nothing is more faith building than seeing that person surrender his or her life to Christ.

Learning to talk with people about spiritual issues is another way to help you acquire Searching Faith. This does not mean using your beliefs as a basis for starting arguments. In fact you should practice communicating with another person on a spiritual subject without letting it digress into an argument. The best place to do this is during church fellowship, at least it should be. During fellowship times, before and after services, learn to ask others about how they are doing spiritually. Find out what others are studying in the Bible and if they are reaching out to any of their friends. Ask if you can be praying for them about anything. There is nothing wrong with talking to Christians about weather, sports, work, etc., but we also need to have the kind of relationships that we can converse on a spiritual plane. If we cannot do that at church where are we going to do it? Talk to brothers about Christ so you can talk to others about Christ.

Another way to help yourself grow as a searcher is to read some good books and listen to some good tapes. Extra-biblical material is not the same as God's inspired Word, but good books can help you explore new ways of thinking about God. Tapes from seminars and workshops can challenge you to look at an old favorite scripture in a new light. If you disagree with the speaker or writer you can search out the reasons why you disagree.

I have read books, some by authors I don't necessarily agree with, and gained insights or learned ministry skills that have been greatly beneficial. When you read books or listen to tapes you want to be open to some different things, but be careful you do not accept ideas that are contrary to God's Word. Do not be too open-minded or your brains will fall out. Anyone with Affiliating Faith needs to avoid questionable books and tapes altogether. They are at greater risk of affiliating with a potentially damaging doctrine.

One of the worst mistakes you can make in regard to your spiritual growth is to wait for someone else to stir you to growth. Take matters into your own hands and be responsible for how you are doing spiritually. "Examine yourselves to see whether you are in the faith; test yourselves. Do you not realize that Christ Jesus is in you—unless, of course you fail the test" (2 Corinthians 13:5). Take personally Paul's admonition to the Corinthians to "Examine yourselves." Don't wait for something to happen. Set out on a course of introspection to see where you are in your relationship to Christ.

Finally, make sure your searching is focused on getting to know Jesus in a deeper way. You need to keep clear in your own mind what you are searching for. The book of Hebrews was written initially for Jewish Christians who had lost sight of their goal. They were even thinking about going back to Judaism. After explaining why it would be spiritual suicide to leave the Christian faith, the Hebrew writer then admonishes, "Let us fix our eyes on Jesus, the author and perfecter of our faith" (12:2). Searching can sometimes lead you off on a wild tangent. Make sure that doesn't happen. Fix your eyes on Jesus. Seek to know Him in a deeper way.

Discussion Questions

1. What is your personal motivation for wanting to grow in your faith?

2. How much does your walk with God depend on the spiritual well being of others?

3. Can you honestly say the things you believe are founded on scripture, the direct Word of God, and not merely the teachings of men (Mark 7:7)?

4. How would reaching out to Non-Christians help you grow in your faith?

5. On a scale of one to ten, how spiritually based would you say your conversation is with other Christians when you attend services?

Chapter Seven

The Struggles of Searching Faith

When we hear the word **struggle,** it generally brings a negative image to our minds. When someone is fighting, we call it a struggle. When an assignment is difficult, we say we are struggling with it. But struggle is not always bad. In fact, it can be good, even quite beneficial. Struggle means we are alive and kicking. Life itself is a struggle. Salmon struggle upstream from the ocean so that they can spawn where their offspring are able to grow up safely. By struggling out of a cocoon, a butterfly develops the strength it needs in its wings so that it can fly. A mother endures the pain of childbirth to bring a new child into the world. Life is about struggle.

God's children have an ongoing struggle against evil. "In your struggle against sin, you have not yet resisted to the point of shedding your blood" (Hebrews 12:4). The Hebrew writer takes for granted that Christians are struggling against sin, because this is what Christians do. If we are not struggling in some way, that is not a good sign. Faith takes effort. "Therefore, my dear friends, as you have always obeyed—not only in my presence, but now much more in my absence—continue to work out your salvation with fear and trembling" (Philippians 2:12).

Searching Faith in particular is impossible to accomplish without some kind of struggle. We don't all wrestle with the same issues, but we do all have our struggles. There are four basic types of struggle one experiences during Searching Faith. By learning these *four basic struggles* you will be able to help yourself understand the course your own searching needs to take and you will be able to assist others better in their search.

The first one (and these are in no particular order), is the *Intellectual Struggle*. This is the struggle to answer the question, Is it true? This was my biggest struggle when I was in college. With a plethora of professors who were evolutionist, humanist, agnostics and pantheists, and I myself coming from an atheistic mindset, I had to have proof of the truths of Christianity. Like Thomas, my attitude was, "Unless I see the nail marks in his hands and put my fingers where the nails were, and put my hand into his side, I will not believe it" (John 20:25).

Are you a Thomas too? Some of us are and some are not. Not everyone struggles intellectually, but if you do the solution is to go ahead and test the Bible. Feel free to put it under the microscope. The Bible will prove itself. It has been doing so for many, many years. If this is your struggle, then search out the answers for yourself so you can be confident that when God is telling you something from His Word it really is God's word, and not just man's (1 Thessalonians 2:13).

Some go through the *Practical Struggle*. This is where you are struggling with whether or not it is practical to follow God. What good is my faith? Does it work when I do things God's way? If I keep turning the other cheek, what will happen to me? Can Christianity honestly help me to be a better athlete, student, employer . . . ? If bad things can still happen to me, what good does it do to follow God? Job was the epitome of the Practical Struggle. (We'll look at Job in depth later on.) The solution to this struggle is to weigh the pros and cons of being a follower of Jesus. Count your blessings and see if the blessings don't far outweigh the inconveniences.

Another common struggle during Searching Faith is the *Emotional Struggle*. This is where we find ourselves emotionally attached to a habit or object and start asking, How can I let go of this? Jesus does not permit us to draw lines in the sand when it comes to following Him. We have to surrender everything into His hands (Luke 14:25-33), but emotionally we want to hold back. It's a struggle. The rich young man had a struggle letting go of his riches (Matthew 19:16-22). Unfortunately, he lost that struggle and walked away from Jesus. The solution to the Emotional Struggle is to apply the faith you have. Try letting go and surrendering to Jesus as much as you can. Trust Him to be your guide. Read what His Word teaches about how to handle certain situations and apply what you learn. When you see how well that works, surrender a little more. Keep doing that until you can surrender it all to Jesus.

The fourth common struggle among searchers is the *Moral Struggle*. This is when one wrestles with the question, Am I too sinful for God? We often feel like we have done things that are so repulsive, there is no way God could ever forgive us. We do not deserve to be forgiven. Even if we are forgiven, Christianity is too hard and we could never change. We might feel the way Peter did when he said, "Go away from me, Lord; I am a sinful man," (Luke 5:8). The solution to the Moral Struggle is to realize that we cannot change but we can be changed. We cannot change ourselves, but God can change us if we will let Him. Whether we understand it or not, God is willing to forgive the vile sins we have committed. Not until we accept His forgiveness are we able to press on.

A similar problem is in refusing to forgive ourselves. Do not set your standards higher than God's. If God can forgive you for that sin you committed, why can't you forgive yourself? Are your righteous standards higher than His? Forgive yourself and move on in your faith.

Is it possible to go through more than one of these struggles when we are searching? Absolutely! You may go through two of them, or three or even all four. But it is impossible to search without going through at least some kind of struggle. If you are just beginning your search, identify the struggle or struggles you are having and work on the solutions to them. It is important to match your path of searching to the struggle you are having.

If you are having an Emotional Struggle, the Intellectual solution will not help you. If you are having a Moral Struggle, establishing the practicality of Christianity is not going to do you much good. Left to your own devices, you will do this automatically. However, others around you may innocently try to steer you a different direction. Your struggles may be different from other disciples you are in contact with, so seek help in the areas where you need to grow the most.

Remember that struggle is good. Think of it as receiving discipline. "No discipline seems pleasant at the time, but painful. Later on, however, it produces a harvest of righteousness and peace for those who have been trained by it" (Hebrews 12:11). Struggle is never pleasant, but the end result, the harvest of righteousness, makes it worth it. Don't lose heart.

Discussion Questions

1. Can you name the four basic struggles of searching faith and briefly explain each one?

2. Do you see how struggle can actually be a good thing? Can you think of any other benefits of struggling?

3. A biblical example was given in this chapter for each of the four struggles. Can you think of more biblical examples?

4. The moral struggle is a difficult one because we are not worthy of God's grace. How would you help someone going through this struggle?

5. Which of these four do you struggle with the most?

Chapter Eight

How Did Peter Search Out His Faith?

Now you have a basic understanding of the five levels of faith and the four struggles of Searching Faith. This is merely terminology unless we learn how to apply these principles to everyday situations. We can gain practical application by studying the examples of biblical characters like Simon Peter. Peter has been kind enough to let us into his life and show us how his faith progressed. Let us take a look.

Peter came to Christ the same way most of us do today. He started with Affiliating Faith. He had his brother, Andrew, to thank for introducing him to Christ (John 1:40-42). Through this sibling affiliation Simon Peter was blessed to make acquaintance with the Savior of the world. From that point on we hear far more about Peter than we do about Andrew. Peter pressed on to become one of the greatest apostles, but we should remember that we would not have Peter if not for his quiet brother who took the time to introduce him to the Lord.

Simon's faith grew quickly and just like the rest of us, he had his struggles. Jesus worked with him and taught him how to bring peace and order into his life through faith. On one occasion a large number of disciples stopped following Jesus in John 6 because they believed His teachings were too hard. Jesus even asked the twelve apostles if they wanted to stop following Him. "You do not want to leave too, do you?" (John 6:67). It was Simon Peter who pointed out, "Lord, to whom shall we go? You have the words of eternal life." (6:68). By this statement it is clear that Peter did not have a Practical Struggle with following Jesus. Peter knew that following the Lord was well worth whatever discomforts or sacrifices he might encounter because Jesus was the only way to achieve the eternal life he desired.

Peter also did not have the Emotional Struggle. After he watched the rich young man walk away from the Lord because he was too emotionally attached to his money, Peter said to Jesus, "We have left everything to follow you," (Mark 10:28). If Peter had trouble giving up something to follow Christ, he had apparently dealt with it by this point. There was nothing in his life that he was so emotionally attached to, he was not willing to part with it for the sake of Christ.

As pointed out in chapter seven, Simon did have a Moral Struggle. The event recorded in Luke 5:1-11 makes this clear. That is when he made the statement, "Go away from me, Lord; I am a sinful man!" Anyone who has been through the Moral Struggle can empathize with the turmoil behind those words. We reach a point where it finally sinks in just whose presence we are in and what He has done for us. If you have ever felt like you are completely unworthy of the goodness you have received from the Lord, undeserving of His precious gift of spiritual cleansing, don't feel alone. Peter has been there too.

What is it about Peter's experience with walking on the water that inspires us so? More sermons have been preached from this text than probably any other in the Bible. It's stirring. It's convicting. It's motivating. He actually walked on top of water. (That is physically impossible, by the way.) Do you have any idea how much faith that takes? Yes, he also faltered at one point. He sank down in the water because his faith wavered. That's true, but he still walked on water. The other apostles didn't even want to get out of the boat, but Peter did. Read the text in Matthew 14:25-31 when you get the chance. It was originally Peter's idea, not Jesus'. He was eager to test his faith. Of all the lessons we could learn from that windy evening on the Sea of Galilee, the most precious one is probably this: Be brave enough to venture out but keep your eyes focused on Jesus. Peter learned a lesson that day about the importance of staying focused.

Another intriguing event in the progress of Peter's growth was the incident in Matthew 16. Jesus was having some "R & R" with the twelve in the northern region of Caesarea Philippi. He asked the question, "Who do people say the Son of Man is?" (16:13). The apostles shared some of the rumors they had heard. It was obvious from these guesses that the commoners still did not know who Jesus was. "But what about you? . . . Who do you say I am?" (16:15). Bet you could have heard a pin drop after Jesus asked that question. It was one thing for the general public not to know who Jesus was, but these men had been following Him for quite some time. They should have had some clue as to who He was. It was Peter who bailed them out. "You are the Christ, the son of the living God." (16:16). Ata boy, Peter! From the response Jesus gives it was obvious He was pleased with Simon Peter. He commended his theistically inspired observation and blessed him. Then six short verses after that Jesus had to rebuke him for being a stumbling block.

As it turned out, Simon was so confident (maybe even a little cocky) from his great accomplishment that when Jesus began to explain how He was going to die in Jerusalem, Simon pulled Him aside to rebuke Him. That's right. Peter was now so spiritual he could even rebuke Jesus Christ. Jesus had to put him in his place again, and we are all privileged to have a little laugh at Peter's expense. But before you laugh too long, consider this. Peter was making some mistakes, but at least he was trying. He had his highs and lows but he was growing because he was putting his faith into practice.

We once had a player on our basketball team who had no turnovers. He never made a bad pass, never even missed a shot. Do you know why? He never played. If you are afraid to make a mistake, the only way to avoid it is to do absolutely nothing. But if you choose to do nothing, do not expect growth in your life. God has a tough time guiding someone who is not moving.

In the next chapter, Matthew 17, Peter, James and John are invited to accompany Jesus up to the Mount of Transfiguration. While on the mountain, Moses and Elijah show up to have a talk with Jesus. Simon Peter has this great idea about building three great monuments to these three great men. God, however, does not think it is a very good idea. Here is what He has to say about Peter's idea: "This is my Son, whom I love; with him I am well pleased. Listen to him!" (17: 5) [Emphasis God's]. What was the message? "You have lost your focus, Peter. Stay focused on my Son, Jesus." Again Peter ventured out. Again Peter was in the wrong, but again Peter learned something.

How about the time Jesus was washing the disciples' feet in the upper room before the Passover? In John 13 the towel clad Master moved meekly from one dirty foot to the next until he came to the soiled soles of Peter. "Lord, are you going to wash my feet?" (13:6). Kind of a silly question, don't you think? Of course He's going to wash his feet. Unless Peter meant, "Lord, are you going to wash MY feet?"

Simon Peter might still be having a Moral Struggle. Here is the King of kings kneeling before him doing the job of a slave. This sounds so much like the inner turmoil Peter faced in Luke 5:8: "Go away from me, Lord; I am a sinful man!" The thought of the Master washing his feet was unbearable. "'No,' said Peter, 'you shall never wash my feet'" (13:8). There, that settles it in Peter's mind, but Jesus will not let him off that easy. "Unless I wash you, you have no part with me" (13:8). Jesus put Peter in a position where he had to face this struggle head on.   Since Jesus was putting it that way, "Then, Lord . . . not just my feet but my hands and my head as well!" (13:9).

Peter. You gotta love him, always swaying from one extreme to the other. Jesus was teaching him, molding him into the pillar of faith he would later become. In the end Jesus washed his feet and Simon Peter learned how to work through the Moral Struggle. That

Moral Struggle is not an easy one to deal with. Sometimes it comes creeping back on you.

It is fascinating to watch the way Jesus shaped and molded Simon. You can tell that Jesus loved this fiery young disciple very much. "Simon, Simon, Satan has asked to sift you as wheat. But I have prayed for you, Simon, that your faith may not fail" (Luke 22:31-32a). Peter's reaction to Jesus' message reminds us so much of ourselves. Rather than thank Jesus for praying for him, he reacted offensively to Jesus' suggestion that his faith might actually fail. "Lord, I am ready to go with you to prison and to death" (22:33). The truth is Peter was not as ready as he thought he was. Even after Jesus told him that he would deny his Lord three times, he did not believe it.

When I teach this material in a seminar setting, one of the first things I do is teach the audience the five levels of faith. After I have explained why I believe the majority of our members are at Affiliating Faith, you can almost read it in their expressions, "Yup, most of these church members are there but I know I am higher than that." Let me caution you, with Peter as an example, do not think of yourself as having a faith more mature than it actually is. You may be dreadfully disappointed with yourself the next time your faith is tested. In order for this study to be of benefit to you, you must be willing to be honest with yourself about where you stand with God.

After Peter finished denying that he even knew Jesus, the Luke account observes that Jesus was looking straight at him. How crushing that must have been. How humiliating. But humility is not a bad thing. It is actually essential to maturing in our faith. Pride weakens our faith. Later when the resurrected Lord asked Peter if he truly loved Him, Peter was guarded, careful not to overstate his loyalty again (John 21:15-17). It is better to think less of yourself than more of yourself. It takes more spiritual maturity to see our own inadequacies and admit we have room to grow. "So, if you think you are standing firm, be careful that you don't fall" (1 Corinthians 10:12).

49

Through the life of Peter we see that spiritual growth is a struggle, but if you have read the book of Acts then you know that in the end the church was richly blessed because Peter was in top spiritual condition. Through the life of Peter we can see how the five levels of faith come into play as well as the four struggles of Searching Faith. Now that you know what to look for, you can identify these stages through the lives of other biblical characters. This will give you a fresh new way to approach your personal Bible study.

Discussion Questions

1. Are there any similarities between the way you came to Christ and the way Simon Peter learned about Jesus?

2. Which of the four struggles of Searching Faith did Simon Peter have the hardest time with?

3. Visualize yourself stepping out of a boat to walk on top of the water. What kind of faith would it take for you to do something like that?

4. In your own life, have you ever felt like you were sinking because you took your eyes off of Jesus?

5. Can you think of any other biblical characters who exemplify the five levels of faith or the struggles of Searching Faith?

Chapter 9

Job and the Practical Struggle

You may have noticed more chapters in this book are devoted to Searching Faith than to the other four levels. The Bible has more examples of Searching Faith than it does of the others. Perhaps this is because the pivotal point of one's spiritual progress is at Searching Faith. It is the point that makes or breaks us as Christians. It is a period of critical transformation as we think and rethink our doctrinal positions and our understanding of who God is and what He wants us to do.

Of the four struggles of Searching Faith, the Practical Struggle is the only one auspicious enough to have an entire book of the Bible devoted to it. The 42 chapters of the book of Job record the Practical Struggle of one man, the questions provoked through his struggle and the way he found his answers. By studying Job, the anatomy of the Practical Struggle rises to the surface and a clear path is laid out showing the way closer to that deep relationship with God which we all long for.

Job loved God. He was by no means perfect, but he went to great lengths to please God as the first five verses of the book indicate. He was wealthy and quite influential in his part of the world, and he used his wealth and his wisdom for the betterment of mankind (Job 4:3-4). His adversary, Satan, despised Job because of his loyalty to the Creator. But Satan believed that Job's faithfulness was the result of his cushy lifestyle, and that if Job were to suffer loss and hardship his faith in God would crumble, proving that evil triumphs over good (1:6-22). After leaving heaven with permission to torment Job, Satan robbed him of his crops, herds, home and children, yet Job did not turn away from God.

In the second chapter of this book, Satan received permission to strike Job's physical health, which he did, causing painful boils to break out all over his body. Job still did not betray God. Satan was wrong. Hardship was not able to dissuade Job from believing in His Creator. But the hardships did cause Job to struggle with the practicality of following the God he loved.

Although Satan was the inflictor of hardship and pain, God was involved and could have stopped this pointless suffering (at least, pointless in Job's mind). Job had obeyed God and yet he still suffered misfortune, which raised the question: what good did it do to follow God, if one still suffers in the process? Was it practical for all intent and purpose to serve the Lord?

To understand the answer to this challenging question we first must be aware of how suffering impacts us spiritually. People react in different ways to misfortune, but there are some common thought processes we experience. If the suffering is taxing enough we sometimes feel like God is pushing us beyond our ability to bear up. Job felt this way and expressed it in chapter six. "What strength do I have, that I should still hope? What prospects, that I should be patient?" (6:11). We generally look for scapegoats to blame for our suffering, as Job did in the next two verses. "A despairing man should have the devotion of his friends, even though he forsakes the fear of the Almighty. But my brothers are as undependable as intermittent streams," (6:14-15). Job took it out on his friends who were supposed to be there to comfort him. Sometimes we use God as our scapegoat, blaming Him for things that cause us hurt and suffering. Interestingly enough, Job did not do this.

Job questioned God, but he never blamed Him for his loss. He wanted to know why God allowed injustice to persist in this world

(12:4-6). Why did righteous people suffer while the ungodly received no apparent punishment for their disobedience? This perception (or misperception) fueled the fire of his Practical Struggle, as did his faulty theology.

The way we perceive God, our theology, has a profound effect on how well we handle the questions surrounding the practicality of Christianity. As you observe the way Job speaks to God in chapter ten verses nine through sixteen, you realize that he sees God as a mean and vindictive God, anxious to punish and slow to forgive. "If I hold my head high, you stalk me like a lion and again display your awesome power against me" (10:16). This is a faulty perception of God. Job's misconception hindered his ability to recover from his loss. Had he known that God is actually "a forgiving God, gracious and compassionate, slow to anger and abounding in love," (Nehemiah 9:17), this would have been a great comfort to him during his time of grief. These things did not happen to Job because God was mad at him. We know that because we have the advantage of listening in on God's conversation with Satan in the first two chapters. God spoke highly of Job's loyalty and righteousness. God loved Job and Job should have known that. Perhaps he simply forgot as we sometimes do.

Eliphaz also had a faulty theology which hindered him from being a comfort to his friend Job. We get the impression from 22:4-10 that Eliphaz believed all suffering was the result of sin. "You gave no water to the weary and you withheld food from the hungry . . . That is why snares are all around you, why sudden peril terrifies you," (22:7, 10). In the opinion of Eliphaz, since Job was suffering it must have been because he sinned. So Eliphaz was trying to get him to 'fess up' when in fact Job's suffering had nothing to do with any sin he had committed.

This was a common Jewish misconception (Luke 13:1-5; John 9:2), and one that unfortunately still exists today. Merely because one suffers does not mean one has sinned. Sin can and does bring about suffering, but the nature of this world dictates that events take place that are not anyone's fault. God is not always trying to punish people with hardship. There are natural occurrences. God is fully capable of overcoming nature. That is true. But just because He chooses not to, does not mean He is deliberately trying to punish someone. Those who don't understand this basic biblical truth suffer needlessly during times of grief. Those in the comforting professions need to understand this basic truth as well.

"How I long for the months gone by, for the days when God watched over me, when his lamp shone upon my head and by his light I walked through darkness!" (29:2-3). What Job is doing in this chapter is reflecting on the good times. This can be very healing for anyone struggling through the practicality of faith in God. Anyone who has tasted the goodness of knowing God can counter attack the negative thoughts of the Practical Struggle by recognizing the worth of following God. Following God is not all rosy. There are difficulties involved, but it is rewarding. And by weighing the pros against the cons we are able to answer the question "Is it worth it to follow God?"

Elihu brings up a good point in chapter thirty-four of Job. "For he says, 'It profits a man nothing when he tries to please God.' So listen to me, you men of understanding. Far be it from God to do evil," (34:9-10). God is not in the business of doing harm or evil to anyone. "God is love" (1 John 4:16). Everything that God does is based on love. So when we lose something that God gave us in the first place He is not being unfair. All that we have truthfully belongs to the Master. We are merely in contact with it for a little while. So if God takes back the wealth He gave us, it was His in the first place and therefore God is not being unjust.

It is our own stubborn pride that causes us to hold on to things that are not rightfully ours. Pride is what makes the Practical Struggle so difficult for us. Job received a healthy dose of humility by the end of his trial and it was the best thing that ever happened in his life. By chapter 42 he understood the sovereignty of God the Father. Then, and only then, did he find the solution to the practical struggle. Is it worth it to follow God? Most definitely! Although things don't always go our way and following God can be difficult at times, in the end it is by far the best life style choice. It is worth any inconvenience we may have to face in this world.

Discussion Questions

1. Why do we find more information in the Bible about Searching Faith than any of the other four?

2. What was the difference between the way God felt about Job and the way Job perceived God's feelings toward him?

3. When you encounter suffering, do you ever catch yourself looking for scapegoats, maybe even blaming God?

4. Is there room in your theology to accept the fact that sometimes things happen and it is not anyone's fault? If not, what scripture would you give to show someone is always responsible?

5. Do you believe Job's suffering was pointless? If not, what did he gain from going through this trial?

Chapter 10

How Do I Start Solidifying My Faith?

Once you have reached the stage of Searching Faith, your next goal should be to get to Solidifying Faith. Solidifying Faith is where you piece together the answers to the questions you have been searching out. In a sense you will always be searching and learning new things, but at some point you have to take what you have learned and make it solid, building the position on which you intend to stand.

Solidifying Faith was something I learned about very early in my own spiritual development, even before I became a Christian. After spending several months studying the Bible and learning what it said about my lost condition, I still had not given my life over to Christ. I remember talking with our preacher one day about his sermon on evangelism. I told him how convicted I was by his message and that I needed to be more active in reaching out to my friends on campus. I was a sophomore in college at the time. I'll never forget his words. "No, Curtis, what *you* need to do is become a Christian yourself." That hurt, but he was absolutely right. Here I was trying to tell others about how wonderful Christianity was. I had actually brought several of my friends to church and Bible study. Some even became Christians before I did. I knew the Word. It was time to decide whether I was going to obey it or not.

When the royal official came to Jesus to ask for the healing of his son, Jesus did not go to see his son but merely said, "You may go. Your son will live." (John 4:50). The text says the official "took Jesus at his word." In other words he believed Jesus. But after he learned for certain that his son was healed, the Bible says, "So he and his whole household believed" 4:53). This man already had belief (faith), but now he took it to the next level. He started solidifying his faith.

In Mark 9 we have another father who wants his son to be healed. This man said to Jesus, "But if you can do anything, take pity on us and help us" (9:22). His words betrayed his lack of faith. He said, "if you can." The statement implied that he had doubts as to Jesus' capabilities. "'Everything is possible for him who believes.' Immediately the boy's father exclaimed, 'I do believe, help me overcome my unbelief.'" (9:23-24). Solidifying our faith is all about overcoming our unbelief. It is not that we do not have faith. We do, but we still have weaknesses in the structure of our faith that need to be shored up or maybe even torn down and reconstructed.

In order to reach Solidifying Faith you must first come to some conclusions. After examining the evidence, what is the verdict? Either you believe it or you do not. That is what you must decide. Are you willing to accept God's will for your life? Paul resisted God's will for a time regarding his "thorn in the flesh". Three times he pleaded with God to remove it. When he realized God was not going to, he resigned himself to God's will (2 Corinthians 12:7-10). This is spiritual maturity. At some point we all have to decide whether we are going to trust God or not, whether we are going to do His bidding or not.

As you are solidifying your faith you also need to realize that some questions may have to go unanswered until we get the opportunity to ask God in eternity. "Where is heaven?" "How could God have no beginning or end?" "Why did God make the pits so big in avocados?" There are certain things you may never find the answer to. The purpose of the Bible is not to answer every question or teach us everything we want to know. It does teach us everything we NEED to know for now. Later on we can learn the rest. For now there are, as Job said, "things to wonderful for me to know" (Job 42:3). An infinite God is difficult to grasp with our finite minds. God's Word teaches us in Deuteronomy 29:29 that there is a certain knowledge that belongs only to God and we need to respect that. It is best for us to remain innocent about some things (Matthew 10:16).

Something we can do to help solidify our faith is pray for a spirit of conviction. There seems to be so little conviction in the church today. Christians are opting for the nominal position of half-hearted allegiance to God. From what I have observed, half-hearted Christianity is an utter waste of time. Jesus explained that the greatest commandment was to "Love the Lord your God with ALL your heart and with ALL your soul and with ALL your mind and with ALL your strength" (Mark 12:30) [Emphasis mine]. One of the best prayers you can pray is to ask God to instill in you a conviction about the Christian campaign we are involved in. The Lord needs warriors who are ready to make Christianity a life commitment instead of a weekend activity.

One last thing that will help you solidify your faith is to start a prayer journal. When we write something down, as opposed to just saying it, we force ourselves to put more thought into it. Also, with a written record of your prayers you can glance back from time to time to see how God is answering you. It is truly a faith-building experience, one that will help you all the more in solidifying your faith.

Before closing this chapter let me caution you. One of the common mistakes made among Christians when it comes to Solidifying Faith is that we tend to want to put a timetable on things. When it comes to spiritual maturity, do not place time restraints on yourself. You cannot say, "By such and such a time I will move on to Solidifying Faith," any more than you can say, "by such and such a time I will be mentally developed or physically taller."

Growth takes time and the best you can do is simply work toward maturity in your personal walk with God and welcome it when it comes. It is good to be eager to grow up spiritually, but it is not wise to overburden yourself with unrealistic expectations. Work on the techniques you are learning in this book and be patient. In this chapter you learned about solidifying your faith by coming to some conclusions about what you do and do not believe. You learned that not all your questions will be answered and in this life you just have to press on without some of those answers. You were encouraged to pray for a spirit of conviction and keep a prayer journal to see how God is answering your prayers. Apply these principles to your life and be patient. The growth will come.

Discussion Questions

1. In your own words, how would you explain the difference between Searching and Solidifying Faith?

2. Do you see why this step is so important on the road to maturity?

3. Is there an unanswered question that is holding you back from experiencing the spiritual growth that should be taking place in your life?

4. Have you ever caught yourself putting time limitations on your spiritual growth?

5. If you do not keep a prayer journal, what would you think about the idea of starting one today?

Chapter 11

Up-Again, Down-Again Faith

"I don't understand myself sometimes. One day I am on fire for the Lord and doing great. The next day I feel like God is a million miles away. What is wrong with me?" Have you ever heard these words, maybe even felt this way yourself? The problem is what I call Up-again, Down-again faith, and you are not alone. Many Christians go through this spiritual roller coaster ride. We all are certain to have our peaks and valleys, our mountain top experiences and our pits of despair. But for some it becomes an addictive cycle.

Everywhere I travel I meet Christians caught up in this cyclone of Up-again, Down-again faith. Each time you talk to them you are not sure which slope they are going to be on next. This predicament was common even among biblical characters.

The first time God called Abram to go, he went. He uprooted his whole family, sold the farm and started down the highway. He did not even know where he was headed, but he went because God said so (Genesis 12:1-4). That's faith. But later on when he was forced into Egypt because of a famine, he feared for his life because his wife Sarai was a beautiful woman, so he lied and said she was his sister (12:10-13). This was not God's plan. He acted contrary to his faith and it resulted in a near catastrophe.

On another occasion when his herdsmen were fighting with Lot's herdsmen over the land, it became obvious they needed to part and go their separate ways. Abram told Lot to choose whatever land he wanted and he would take what was left to him (13:5-12). Abram did so in faith knowing that God had promised him all the land of Canaan. Now his faith was up again.

Then later down the road, God promised him numerous offspring. The only problem was Sarai had not had any children, so the two of them decided to help God out. Abram got Hagar pregnant, who was Sarai's maidservant. This was another spiritual valley for Abram. He did not trust God. And so we see Abram's faith going up and down throughout the Bible.

There are other biblical examples as well. The Israelites as a nation suffered from Up-again, Down-again faith. When Moses led them out of Egypt their faith in God was at an all-time high. God had delivered them after more than six hundred years of bondage. But when they saw themselves trapped against the Red Sea they were angry at God for not leaving them in Egypt. In such a short time their faith plummeted to nearly nothing. Then when Moses parted the Red Sea the Israelites once again trusted God and walked through on a dry sea floor. Think about that one for a minute. That took some faith. But later when they realized they were running out of water in the Sinai Peninsula they lost their confidence in God. You can trace this pattern of highs and lows all the way through the Bible with the Israelites.

Let us look at a third example. You can see this pattern of Up-again, Down-again faith with Elijah who faithfully and boldly challenged 850 false prophets of Baal and Asherah to a sacrifice showdown. He confidently defeated these pagan worshippers by trusting God. But shortly after this he ran scared for his life from a single woman named Jezebel (1Kings 18-19). Or how about John the Baptist, whom we see confidently proclaiming that Jesus is the prophesied Messiah (John 1:29-34). Later on, however, he is asking, "Are you the one who was to come, or should we expect someone else?" (Matthew 11:3).

In most of these cases of Up-again, Down-again faith you could argue that circumstances had an impact on how strong their faith was. Granted, but should circumstances dictate the strength of our

Christian faith? As was pointed out in the last chapter we either believe God and trust Him or we do not. The circumstances we find ourselves in can and do change at any time. But true faith is not swayed by one's circumstances. Our faithless nose-dives have more to do with the preparation and the choices we make than they do with our surroundings.

Mature Faith does not waiver with changing circumstances, but rather holds firm in the fiery onslaught of Satan's attacks. Those, however, who do not solidify their faith as we discussed in chapter ten, are vulnerable to the terrorist style attacks of Satan and his cohorts. There are spiritual choices we make that weaken our defensive position and cause our faith to waiver.

One thing we do to cause Up-again, Down-again faith is we set ourselves up for disappointment. We do this first of all by having a *false expectation of ourselves*. When that frustrated father brought his demon possessed son to Jesus' disciples to be healed in Mark 9, the disciples honestly thought they could heal him. Their unsuccessful attempts to heal the boy only served to further frustrate this father. "I asked your disciples to drive out the spirit, but they could not," (9:18). The apostles set themselves up for disappointment because they had a false expectation of their own abilities.

The father also set himself up for disappointment because he *had a false expectation of others.* When you put your confidence in what others are going to do for you, you run the risk of facing disappointment. We must learn to trust people without putting our trust in people. Do not set yourself up for some disillusionment that will lead you to Up-again, Down-again faith.

You can even set yourself up for disappointment by *having a false expectation of God.* When you decide God is obligated to do certain things that He never promised He would do, then you put yourself in a precarious position. "God is going to give me what I am requesting and if he doesn't . . . " When things do not happen the way you think they should, you are sure to be frustrated and your faith will falter.

A fourth cause of Up-again, Down-again faith *is **not having our doubts removed through endurance.*** "[T]he testing of your faith develops perseverance. Perseverance must finish its work so that you may be mature and complete, not lacking anything" (James 1:3-4). The experience of going through a trial and relying on God to get you through it, gives you the stability you need so that you do not stumble every time a temptation comes along.

Sometimes Up-again, Down-again faith is the result of ***un-dealt with sin in our lives.*** Bring to your mind for a moment Jesus' *Parable of the Sower.* The farmer scattered seed on various types of soil. One was the rocky soil. "The one who received the seed that fell among the rocky places is the man who hears the word and at once receives it with joy. But since he has no root, he lasts only a short time. When trouble or persecution comes because of the word, he quickly falls away" (Matthew 13:20-21).

We are not told what the rocks in the soil represent in this parable. We know that rocks have to be removed from soil before planting in order for the roots of the plants to grow deep. Since the soil represents our hearts and the seed represents God's Word, sin is a strong parallel to the rocks in this parable. We know we need to remove sin from our hearts so that God's Word will sink deep into our lives. When we hold back on dealing with certain "pet" sins, God's Word is only able to grow in us until sin stops it. Sin stops God's Word from taking a deep root in our lives. Then "[w]hen trouble or persecution comes" we experience Up-again, Down-again faith.

Sixth, and finally, this condition can be caused by ***distractions in our lives***. This same parable of the sower talks about "the worries of this life and the deceitfulness of wealth" (13:22). Worldliness restrains us from having a steady walk with God. We get too worried about the bills, sports, TV programs, computers, cell phones, jobs, and so on, to keep our focus on the things that are really important. In this 21st century there are so many worldly things competing for our time and attention. It is difficult to stay focused on our Lord. We focus for a while and then something comes along that needs our urgent attention. After the distraction is dealt with, we come back to the Lord. Then we get preoccupied once more. The result is speed-up, slow-down Christianity, Up-again, Down-again faith. It is enough to make you spiritually car sick. The cure keeps your priorities straight. Do not get caught up in the things of this world.

These are the things that cause Up-again, Down-again faith. So what is the cure? If you know the causes you can head off these obstacles in your life and smooth out the humps. As was mentioned before, you are going to have your good days and your bad days. That is understandable. But what you want to avoid is a pattern of spiritual climbs and dives that never seem to get better. If you see this happening in your life right now then study and take to heart the advice in this chapter. Get off the roller coaster so you can make smooth, steady progress in your spiritual maturity.

Discussion Questions

1. Can you think of any other biblical examples of Up-again, Down-again faith?

2. How much do you let circumstances dictate how strong your faith is?

3. Can you see in your own life how worldly temptations compete for your time, time you could spend growing closer to God?

4. Have you ever set yourself up for disappointment by having a false expectation of yourself, others or God?

5. How do you plan to put what you have learned in this chapter into practice?

Chapter 12

What's So Great About Abraham's Faith?

Christians pray for the patience of Job and the faith of Abraham. But what was so great about Abraham's faith? He had his faithless moments as we have already studied. He was, at times, apathetic to the will of God and self-reliant. What was it about this man that gained him the reputation of having such great faith?

Let us first understand that when Abraham is referred to as the "father of our faith" this is not necessarily a reference to the degree of faithfulness that he obtained. There is another definition of faith used in the Bible - one which we did not deal with in chapter two. Faith can also mean a system of religious beliefs. Abraham was the "father of our faith" in the sense that he was the origin of both the Judeo/Christian and Islamic religions. These two religions refer to Abraham as their religious father when they call him the father of their faith. Nevertheless, Abraham was a man of exemplary faith.

As we discovered in the last chapter, Abraham was willing to leave the comfort of his native land when God called him to uproot. He was commended for this in Hebrews 11:8-10. The Bible says, "(He) obeyed and went, even though he did not know where he was going." Keep in mind that Abraham was a farmer. Farmers just don't up and leave to a new place very easily. What he did took notable faith. Unlike the children of God who move around today, his move was based purely on spiritual reasons. "For he was looking forward to a city with foundations, whose architect and builder is God" (11:10).

When we make decisions to move nowadays it is often based on financial, physical or familial reasons. We hardly consider whether God wants us to make the move or not, whether there will be a strong church at the new location or whether our family will do well spiritually. We follow the money and hope God will be there when we arrive. Abraham did not make his relocation based on worldly reasons.

Abraham had great faith because he took God at His word. "Abram believed the Lord, and he credited it to him as righteousness" (Genesis 15:6). God said it. That settled it. The context for this verse is God promising him that his descendants would be numerous. Abraham believed even though he did not know how God was going to accomplish His promise. As we witnessed in the last chapter, Abraham even tried to aid God in fulfilling His promise by impregnating Hagar, which was wrong of him to do. But he did not at any point doubt that God would somehow do what He said He would do.

Abraham's faith was also great because of the way he passed his beliefs on to his children. I remember watching a television special about Abraham on PBS one night. It showed him spending hours and hours with Isaac trying to teach him the ways of Jehovah. He was doing what God commanded him to do in Genesis 18:18-19. Those who strive to pass their faith on to their children show how deeply they care about their children and their beliefs. Any father or mother who teaches their children to serve God faithfully exemplifies their own great faith.

Abraham also had the kind of faith that motivated him to intercede on the behalf of others. When the Lord shared with him what He was planning to do to Sodom and Gomorrah, Abraham pleaded for those people. "What if there are fifty righteous people in the city? Will you really sweep it away and not spare the place for the sake of the fifty righteous people" (18:24). He bargained with

God all the way down to ten righteous people. Just pause and think about this for a minute. Do you think you could honestly carry on so bold a conversation as this with the Almighty? It makes me shudder to think about it. Only a child of God with great faith could speak with God in such a way. His great faith allowed Abraham to have such a relationship with the Heavenly Father.

Because of his faith, Abraham was able to see so many wonderful works of the Great "I AM". He witnessed the miraculous birth of his son Isaac - a child born when both he and Sarah were way past the age of childbearing. This happened because of his faith according to Hebrews 11:11-12. Then one of the ultimate tests of Abraham's faith was when God told him to offer up his son, his only son, Isaac. There was nothing on earth Abraham loved and cherished more than Isaac. God could not have given him a more difficult test, but Abraham passed the test. He did exactly as the Lord asked him to do, to the point that God had to stop his hand. When you are ready to give up your most prized possession whenever God asks it of you, then you know your faith is great.

Abraham was far from being a perfect man, but he trusted God. Praying for the faith of Abraham is a blessed thing to pray for. Abraham was blessed because he trusted Jehovah enough to follow His guidance. That is what faith is all about. Studying the faith of characters in the Bible like Abraham gives us a wealth of insight into what God expects of us. God truly does love you. He recognizes and rewards your efforts to serve Him.

Discussion Questions

1. Do you still remember what your motivation is for wanting to grow in your faith?

2. What do we mean when we refer to Abraham as the father of our faith?

3. The last time you moved, what was the reason for moving? Did you take into consideration whether God wanted you to make that move or not?

4. Can you picture yourself standing face to face with God bargaining for the lives of the people of Sodom? What kind of faith would it take for you to do something like that?

5. If God asked you right now to give up something or someone that you love dearly, could you do it?

Chapter 13

Can I Reach Mature Faith?

It never fails. Every time I try to talk to Christians about having mature faith there are those who believe mature faith is some lofty, unattainable plateau that they will never reach. Where does that mindset come from? It certainly does not come from scripture.

The scriptures emphasize, even demand, spiritual maturity. We have already discussed Matthew 17:14-20. God wants our mustard seed faith to grow. James 1:2-8 explains how trials are good because they eventually lead to our maturity. "Perseverance must finish its work so that you may be mature and complete, not lacking anything" (1:4). In Colossians 4:12 we find that Epaphras is praying for the faith of the brethren in Colosse that they may reach maturity. And the Hebrew writer is vividly disappointed at the lack of growth he is seeing in the Christians he addresses.

"We have much to say about this, but it is hard to explain because you are slow to learn. In fact, though by this time you ought to be teachers, you need someone to teach you the elementary truths of God's word all over again. You need milk, not solid food! Anyone who lives on milk, being still an infant, is not acquainted with the teaching about righteousness. But solid food is for the mature, who by constant use have trained themselves to distinguish good from evil" (Hebrews 5:11-14).

Throughout God's Word we are urged to strive for maturity. Now wouldn't God be a cruel God to urge us to obtain the unobtainable? Mature faith is a reachable goal or our Father would not even ask it of us.

Mature faith often appears to be out of reach because of the following misconceptions. First, *we are looking at our own strength* instead of relying on the strength of the Almighty. When I see nothing but myself, I feel helpless to achieve any spiritual progress. But when I look to God to work through me, there is no mountain too high to climb. That is why when Gideon went out to fight the Midianites with 32,000 men God did not want them to think the battle was going to be won by their own strength, so he had Gideon sift through the men sending them home until he had 300 left. Then they fought the battle (Judges 7). On your own, you will not reach mature faith. But put your trust in God and He can lead you to the spiritual level you need to be at.

A second misconception for why we do not think Mature Faith is obtainable is because *we equate it with sinless perfection*. Think about it. Abraham had mature faith. So did Noah, Samuel, Paul, etc. Were they sinlessly perfect? No. They were mature, but not perfect. At least not in the way we mean "perfect". You may already know that the Greek word for "mature" can also be translated "perfect" (i.e. Matthew 5:48; 19:21; Romans 12:2; 1 Corinthians 2:6; 13:10; 14:20; Ephesians 4:13; Philippians 3:15; Colossians 1:28; 4:12; Hebrews 5:14; 9:11; James 1:4,17,25; 3:2; 1 John 4:18). Now if you just glanced at that list of scriptures without looking them up (as I often do when I am reading), let me encourage you to take out your Bible and look each one of them up. I know it is a fairly long list but reading them will in itself answer your question about what it means to be mature. As these verses show, many throughout the New Testament not only were encouraged to strive for maturity/perfection/ *telios*, but there were a number who were accredited with having already obtained it (Philippians 3:15; 1 Corinthians 2:6). Since Jesus was the only one to walk this earth without having sinned, we must conclude that this maturity is something that can be obtained and that it is not equivalent with being absolutely free from sin. So when we talk about having mature faith we are talking about a reachable goal.

One last misconception on why many are afraid to strive for Mature Faith is that *they believe by obtaining it they might become prideful*. There is no reason to worry about this because the one actually excludes the other. The very process of striving to know God in a deeper way strains all the prideful and haughty attitudes right out of your heart. It is like passing through a sifter. Remember that pride leads us away from God. Humility leads to maturity and intimacy with the Father. If and when you reach Mature Faith, you will not find any pride there. When you bask in pride you forfeit spiritual maturity.

Mature Faith is certainly a plateau that you and I can reach with the help of God. I hope that you find great encouragement in this fact. As a child of God you should have your sights set on the highest level of spiritual maturity you can possibly attain. Do not let a faulty understanding of this term keep you from pressing on toward the goal.

Discussion Questions

1. What do you think it means to have Mature Faith?

2. Was there anything mentioned in this chapter that swayed your view of what Mature Faith actually means?

3. Do you believe it is possible to jump from Imitating or Affiliating Faith right to Mature Faith?

4. Why is it possible to have Mature Faith without being sinlessly perfect?

5. Do you honestly believe you can reach Mature Faith?

Chapter 14

How Do I Reach Mature Faith?

Now that we have established that we can indeed reach Mature Faith, let us look at what the Bible has to say about obtaining it. There *are six facets of reaching Mature Faith* which we will be discussing in this chapter. Each one will be shown with its scriptural reference. By going through the other four levels of faith we have discussed many steps that lead to maturity, but the ones in this chapter are for those who have obtained Solidifying Faith and are prepared to go on to maturity.

The first facet: when the Hebrew writer rebukes the Israelite Christians for their immaturity, he explains that, "In fact, though by this time you ought to be teachers, you need someone to teach you the elementary truths of God's word all over again" (5:12). Apparently spiritual maturity has a great deal to do with *becoming a teacher* of the gospel. One sign of physical maturity is reaching the point where you no longer have to be spoon-fed, but rather are able to help others eat. In the same way, being able to feed spiritual food to others is a mature thing to do.

One of the most enriching studies of God's Word I have ever done is a study of the concept of being fruitful. On the one hand, bearing fruit sounds like something you do within yourself; the fruits of the Spirit in Galatians 5. On the other hand, fruitfulness seems to have an evangelistic ring to it, as in Colossians 1:6. When you put both hands together, the conclusion is that bearing fruit has to do with reproducing Christ, both in our own lives and also in the lives of others. Being mature involves being fruitful in the fullest sense of the word. If you want to have Mature Faith, it is essential that you find a way to teach God's Word both to yourself and to others.

Second, the same passage says that, "solid food is for the mature, who by constant use have trained themselves to distinguish good from evil" (5:14). Another key to maturity is *training yourself to know right from wrong*. You do this by "constant use," trying and applying your faith over and over. Train yourself by your daily experience to perpetually seek that which is good and true while at the same time ridding evil from your life. Think of an athlete in training. Athletes work on their skills over and over until they become second nature. To become a mature Christian, you must be able to distinguish good from evil in your own life and also in the lives of others.

The third facet leading to Mature Faith is *letting go of worldly passions* (1 John 2:15-17). As long as you are emotionally attached to your worldly possessions, Satan has a way to distract and frustrate you. If you love your money, boats, cars, houses, etc., and place them above God and His kingdom, they will be a constant thorn in your side as you strive for a closer walk with God. In my research I have talked to many Christians who are considered by their peers as having spiritual maturity. They are, without exception, the most non-worldly people you will meet. Some are rich and some are poor, but each sees the things of this world for what they truly are. These are items that will some day perish. If you are still emotionally attached to your toys, it's time to put things in perspective and start growing up in your faith.

This leads to our fourth facet. If you want to have Mature Faith you need *to stop acting like a child*. That is what Paul was trying to teach us in 1 Corinthians 13:9-12. "When I was a child, I talked like a child, I thought like a child, I reasoned like a child. When I became a man, I put childish ways behind me" (13:11). If you want to be mature you need to stop acting like a spoiled child whenever you don't get your way. The leaders of your church are not responsible for appeasing everyone and keeping all the members content, like babies in a nursery. Their job is to help you grow up (Ephesians 4:11-13). An eagle will push her eaglets out of the nest when the right time comes. It sounds cruel but it is necessary or the eaglets will not learn how to fly. Do you have a church leader who is nudging you to try out your wings? Rather than giving that minister or elder a hard time you should be thanking God for them. Put the childish ways behind you.

A fifth facet of maturing spiritually is that you have *to forget the past and press on*. As Paul was striving for maturity in Philippians 3:12-15, he shared about the struggle he had in forgetting his haunting past: "But one thing I do: Forgetting what is behind and straining toward what is ahead" (3:13). Paul once devoted his life to putting a stop to the Christian movement. He ordered Christians to their death. (And you thought your past was difficult to overcome.) The past can weigh us down. We all have skeletons in the closet reminding us of a time when we lived in disobedience to our Creator. There is nothing you or I can do about the past. If we don't forgive ourselves for things we have done, the past will become a ball and chain preventing us from running free in Christ.

The sixth and final biblical facet of maturity is somewhat a repeat of the first point. It has to do with *learning to share our faith*. All the examples of spiritual maturity that I know of in the Bible are soul-winners. Paul's goal was to "win as many as possible" (1 Corinthians 9:19). Of the many Christians I have talked to who are considered the most mature by their congregations, every one of them is active in leading others to Christ. I believe there is a double-edged reason for this. On one side, there is nothing more faith building and encouraging than watching someone you have shared the gospel with come to Christ. When you teach the gospel to others it matures your own faith. On the other side, the more mature you are in your faith the more desire you have to want to see others partake of the salvation you have found. As you become more mature spiritually you naturally become more evangelistic. Sharing your faith spawns a cycle of growth that is a wonder to behold.

God's Word shows you a clear path to the spiritual plane He wants you to be on. Most of us as Christians have no idea how strong our walk with God could be. We hold back, for God-only-knows what reason. If you will patiently and persistently follow these guidelines you can and will reach Mature Faith. You know it is God's will for you to become more mature. Now you need to make it your will as well.

Discussion Questions

1. Without looking back, how many of the six facets for obtaining Mature Faith can you list?

2. Have you ever studied the concept of being fruitful? If so, have you noticed the two-fold manner in which this term is presented in scripture?

3. We are commanded in 1 John 2:15, "Do not love the world." How attached are you to this material world?

4. Have you experienced problems with the past holding you back from being effective for Christ?

5. When was the last time you felt the faith-building joy of seeing a soul come to Christ through your personal ministry? In what way does that experience reaffirm your convictions for the cause of Christ?

Chapter Fifteen
How Does Satan Attack Faith?

Satan is not stupid. I can assure you he knows exactly what he is doing. He has a plan for bringing you down (Ephesians 6:11). He is relentless and he knows your weaknesses. Since faith is "being sure of what we hope for and certain of what we do not see" (Hebrews 11:1), then all Satan has to do is make you unsure or uncertain. He does not have to destroy your faith to win the battle. He only has to compromise you and when he does he has won and you have lost.

When I was playing basketball we used to get scouting reports on the opposing teams. We needed to know their weaknesses and strengths, where they had their success in winning games and how they could be defeated. This was valuable information. If their strengths were able to exploit our weaknesses then we knew what we needed to work on in practice that week. The same thing is true with Satan.

You need to know what his objective is and where he is vulnerable because you are in a war for your soul. His whole objective is to get you to compromise your faith. He strives to weaken your faith by sending counter-productive messages through television, education, music, friends and even family. He will use any tool he can to plant seeds of doubt in your mind. He doesn't even have to get you to stop attending church. His goal is for you to have stagnant faith, no growth, no reaching out. He wins if he gets you to settle for nominal church attendance.

So let's take a close look at the enemy and his helpers. We know from scripture that Satan is in the business of ***providing temptation***. He cannot make us sin but he can make sure we have ample opportunity to do so. He is even called "the tempter" when he tempts Jesus in Matthew 4. In this passage we have the tempter offering things to Jesus that sounded attractive but resulted in sin and disobedience to the Father. "If you are the Son of God, tell these stones to become bread" (4:3). We will have temptations in the areas we are weakest in. When you conquer and overcome a temptation in your life Satan tries something else. He is not so ignorant as to try to tempt you in something you do not have a struggle with.

If Satan knows you struggle with sexual lust, then that is the area he will target. This has been one of his favorites for years, and he has a new weapon he has added to his arsenal. It is called internet pornography. It is easily accessible and nobody even has to know you are doing it. It fits perfectly with what Satan is trying to accomplish, but beware. Once you start down that path it is a wicked habit to break.

As a minister working with college students I have had the displeasure of counseling a number of young people addicted to pornography. In every case I know of it has led to physical sexual immorality. We take too lightly the urges and compulsions we are dealing with in this realm. Many a Christian who believed they were "strong enough to handle it," found out they were just as vulnerable as anyone else. I am begging you, if you are being tempted by pornography, whether it be from the internet, magazines, videos, whatever, please get help from a church leader. It will totally destroy your relationship with God unless you stop it.

Satan also attacks our faith by *providing hardships*. We learned that from Job in chapter nine. If Satan believes you can be led astray through hard times, that is what he will use. Picture a young committed couple who falls into financial hardship. She gets a job to help make ends meet. Maybe he gets a second job. Before long they don't have time to read the Bible or pray together like they used to. One or both of them gets scheduled to work on Sundays or Wednesday nights. Before long they are not getting the spiritual nourishment they need for a healthy and vibrant walk with God and they begin to wither on the vine. Satan has once again done his job.

Or picture a couple with a young child. They love their child deeply but one day that child is taken away by death. Seeds of doubt come as a result of this hardship. "If God really loved us, why would He allow our baby to be taken away?" That is a tough one. Satan will use it if he thinks it will pull us away from God.

The other side of the coin is Satan can attack our faith by *providing affluence*. I have seen this one many times. Your company offers you a promotion, but it means locating to a place where there is no church or where you and your family will not do well spiritually. Or through your affluence you become pridefully independent, feeling like maybe you don't need God as much in your life. Affluence can be a curse rather than a blessing. I like what Agur the son of Jakeh had to say about this subject. "Give me neither poverty nor riches, but give me only my daily bread. Otherwise, I may have too much and disown you and say, 'Who is the Lord?' Or I may become poor and steal, and so dishonor the name of my God." (Proverbs 30:8-9). When was the last time you turned down a job because it offered too much money? Be careful. Satan can work through affluence to pull you away from God.

Sometimes Satan attacks our faith by *providing destructive messages* - particularly with regards to home and family. See if you recognize some of his messages. "Marriage doesn't have to last a life time. If your marriage isn't working, just get a divorce." "Sexual purity and virginity is boring. Get out and live it up." "No one needs to be the head of the household." "The Bible was great during its time, but it just doesn't apply today." These thoughts do not come from God. They are messages from Satan and he uses them to weaken our faith.

One final trick of the Devil is he sometimes leads us to believe *that talk can take the place of action*. We can talk all we want about being pure, but until we take action against our sin nothing is different. We can talk about evangelism and all the different ways to get it done, but until we actually do it, nobody gets saved. Talk is cheap. "Suppose a brother or sister is without clothes and daily food. If one of you says to him, 'Go, I wish you well; keep warm and well fed,' but does nothing about his physical needs, what good is it?" (James 2:15-16). James makes a good point here. What good is it? Do not be fooled. Do not live in the land of good intentions. Stop merely talking about living God's way and start doing it.

This is spiritual warfare, and Satan is out to tear down your faith. Don't let him. If you lose your faith, you lose your most precious possession so guard it carefully. Don't let Satan have any victories in your life. This chapter shows only a few of Satan's tactics. It is up to you to figure out how he is getting to you. If you rely on God you have nothing to fear from Satan. Keep your guard up, resisting Satan's deceptive strikes. If you do he will flee from you (James 4:7).

Discussion Questions

1. Have you ever participated in a sport where the scouting report was helpful to you?

2. How has Satan been tempting you lately and what are you doing to counter that temptation?

3. In the area of sexual temptations, what are you doing to keep your mind pure and focused on God?

4. If you are not content with your income, do you see how Satan can manipulate your dissatisfaction for his own twisted purpose?

5. In a practical way, what are some steps you can take this week to guard your faith against Satan's attacks?

Chapter 16

Do I Trust God?

In the end, this is what it boils down to. Do I trust God? Faith is seeking the truthful answer to this question. Am I willing to place my life in His hands? Am I going to stand on the promise that my Heavenly Father will do what He said He was going to do? This is what God has wanted His children to do from the beginning.

When Jehovah directed Moses to lead the Israelite nation out of Egypt into the desert of Shur, they were completely dependent on God for everything. The only water that was available was bitter, non-consumable. Certainly this would have discouraged many a weary traveler, but it was nothing God could not handle. God changed the water so they could drink it. What was His message: "Trust me!"

Then they needed food. God provided manna. It simply fell from the sky. All they had to do was go out and pick it up. He told the Israelites to only gather enough for one day because the next day He would provide for them again. Did they trust Him? Did they only gather enough for one day like He said? No! They gathered extra just in case God couldn't handle providing for His children two days in a row. Overnight the manna spoiled and it was so full of maggots the people had to throw it out.

Then on the sixth day God told them to gather enough for two days because He was not going to send food on the Sabbath. They did so and the manna did not spoil overnight. What was the point of this whole exercise? God is saying, "TRUST ME!"

How about it? Do you trust God? As we draw this study to a close it is time to be painfully honest with ourselves. God's kingdom is desperately in need of disciples who are truly FAITH-FULL. He doesn't need any more of the quasi-religious. The world is full of people like that. The church needs men and women who are sincerely godly, who trust the Father implicitly and stand on His precepts. Do you fit this model? The following six statements are a test of faith. Read and consider each one carefully. Decide whether each one is a statement you can make in all good conscience.

- I TRUST GOD to forgive me for everything I have done. I also forgive myself.

- I TRUST GOD to forgive my brother for everything he has done. I also forgive my brother.

- I TRUST GOD'S ways over my own. I will obey Him even when things don't go my way.

- I TRUST GOD to set the standards and guidelines for all of my relationships.

- I TRUST GOD to place me wherever He wants me. I will be content with whatever circumstances He puts me in.

- I TRUST GOD with all that I am and all that I have. Every day, I place my life in His hands.

No matter what level of faith you are at right now, no matter what type of struggle you are going through, trust God. Learn to trust Him more and more. You now know how to recognize where you are at in your walk with God so you can visualize what it is going to take to become mature in your faith. It is my prayer that you will use this material first to improve your walk with God and secondly to assist others to grow in their faith.

Whenever I read a book like this one, I often find myself wishing I could speak with the author to ask questions or get further information. I want you to know that I am willing to make myself as available as I possibly can to help you with any questions you may have. I have dedicated my life to the spiritual development of others and if there is anything I can do to help you grow closer to God I am more than happy to help. Please feel free to contact me.

I pray that God will bless you richly in your search for deeper faith. Trust God. Lean on His word. Pray always and grow in your faith.

Curtis Hartshorn is currently ministering with the Church of Christ in Alamosa, Colorado. He has been there since 1999 working primarily with the college students. He directs the evangelistic Bible studies on campus and is chaplain for several of the athletic teams. He has also taught courses for the college on *Principles of Marriage* and *Death and Dying*. He is the chaplain for the sheriff's department, providing Biblical Counseling for both the inmates and jail staff, and has written various Christian education materials. Brother Hartshorn has been preaching for the Lord's church since 1987. His Bachelor of Arts degree is in English and he has a Master of Biblical Studies from Bear Valley Bible Institute of Denver with an emphasis in Biblical Counseling. He and his lovely wife Kathy have three children; Mario, Tony and Branson.